CHICA

THE CITY A

Lake Point Tower
Still a desirable address five decades on, Lake
Point has great lake views and its own park.
See p069

John Hancock Center
SOM's glowering, charismatic skyscraper
signposts the start of the Magnificent Mile.
See p065

Aqua Tower
Stunning when seen from the street, this 2010
high-rise is an exemplar of sustainable design.
See p075

Aon Center
A strict, severe but rather lovely tower
looming to the north of Millennium Park.
See p013

Trump Tower
Hiring architect Adrian Smith to design his
92-storey downtown leviathan was one of the
business magnate's smartest moves.
See p068

Marina City
Bertrand Goldberg's buildings are charming
concrete remnants of 1960s idealism.
See p015

Chicago Board of Trade
The architectural jewel of the commerce
corridor is this 1930 art deco masterpiece.
141 W Jackson Boulevard

Willis Tower
Overtaken as America's tallest building by One
World Trade Center in NYC, Willis remains one
 the world's most elegant mega-structures.
 e p012

INTRODUCTION
THE CHANGING FACE OF THE URBAN SCENE

Despite the lure of its suburbs (which still threaten to entice inner-city dwellers), Chicago remains in the ascendant. The 'city of broad shoulders' – a place associated with political cynicism, organised crime, music (blues and jazz, perhaps the truest of American art forms) and architecture at its most adventurous – is once again a confident, hopeful place, in large part because of the ingenuity of its entrepreneurs and creative community.

Chicago is the most American of America's metropolises, and it has paid for it. Once a rival to New York, it suffered in comparison to Gotham the global city, then felt the pain as Los Angeles' glitter eclipsed its meat and smoke. Now, interesting because it is not LA or NYC, Chicago has reinvented itself. Formerly hog butcher to the world, it's currently one of the cleanest and most attractive places in the US. It is true that The Loop is an unusual proposition. Look skywards and you'll see the iconography of civic ambition. Down on the street, there are shabby storefronts, ill-designed condos and, often, conspicuous poverty. But in front is Millennium Park (sec p066), a public space of radical intention. Regeneration has run its course in Bucktown and Wicker Park, but this has allowed districts like Pilsen, Logan Square and Avondale, all now filling up with shops, bars and restaurants, to come into their own.

Chicago is still working out how it gets from what it was to what it wants to be, and that is what makes it truly invigorating.

ESSENTIAL INFO
FACTS, FIGURES AND USEFUL ADDRESSES

TOURIST OFFICE
Choose Chicago
77 E Randolph Street
www.choosechicago.com

TRANSPORT
Airport transfer to city centre
Blue line trains depart regularly, 24 hours
a day. The journey takes about 40 minutes
www.transitchicago.com/airports
Car hire
Avis
214 N Clark Street
T 312 782 6825
www.avis.com
Taxis
Chicago Carriage Cab Co
T 312 326 2221
Trains
Chicago Transit Authority
T 312 836 7000
www.transitchicago.com
Red and Blue lines run a 24-hour service;
all other lines run from approximately
5am to 1.30am
Travel card
A CTA day pass is $10, or $28 for seven days

EMERGENCY SERVICES
Emergencies
T 911
24-hour pharmacy
Walgreens
641 N Clark Street
T 312 587 1416

CONSULATE-GENERAL
British Consulate-General
Suite 2200
625 N Michigan Avenue
T 312 970 3800
www.gov.uk/government/world/usa

POSTAL SERVICES
Post office
540 N Dearborn Street
T 312 644 3919
Shipping
UPS
T 312 917 1705

BOOKS
Chicago Makes Modern edited by
Mary Jane Jacob and Jacquelynn Baas
(University of Chicago Press)
**The Chicagoan: A Lost Magazine of
the Jazz Age** by Neil Harris
(University of Chicago Press)
The Man with the Golden Arm
by Nelson Algren (Seven Stories Press)

WEBSITES
Architecture
www.architecture.org
Newspaper
www.chicagoreader.com

EVENTS
Chicago Design Harvest
www.design-harvest.com
Open House Chicago
www.openhousechicago.org

COST OF LIVING
**Taxi from O'Hare International
Airport to city centre**
$60
Cappuccino
$4
Packet of cigarettes
$10
Daily newspaper
$2
Bottle of champagne
$60

CHICAGO
Population
2.7 million
Currency
US dollar
Telephone codes
USA: 1
Chicago: 312/773
Local time
GMT -6
Flight time
London: 8 hours

Montreal
Boston
Toronto
New York
ILLINOIS
Chicago
Washington DC

AVERAGE TEMPERATURE / °C

| 40 |
| 30 |
| 20 |
| 10 |
| 00 |
| -10 |
| -20 | J F M A M J J A S O N D |

AVERAGE RAINFALL / MM

| 140 |
| 120 |
| 100 |
| 080 |
| 060 |
| 040 |
| 020 | J F M A M J J A S O N D |

NEIGHBOURHOODS
THE AREAS YOU NEED TO KNOW AND WHY

To help you navigate the city, we've chosen the most interesting districts (see below and the map inside the back cover) and colour-coded our featured venues, according to their location; those venues that are outside these areas are not coloured.

THE LOOP

The centre is the heart of the architects' playground – innumerable skyscrapers cluster in-between Millennium Park (see p066) to the east and the Chicago River and the financial district to the west. The L train clatters overhead, providing the best viewing platform, while drab chain stores proliferate at ground level.

LINCOLN PARK

For the past 30 years, this comfortable residential zone, named after Chicago's largest park, has been inhabited by the young monied folk. W Armitage Avenue has a concentration of once-cool retail and eating opportunities, now put in the shade by Wicker Park and the West Loop.

SOUTH LOOP

After decades in the doldrums, the South Loop has gentrified, via loft conversions and destination restaurants like Acadia (see p061). Many streets are still lined by the imposing warehouses that formed the backdrop to Al Capone's misdemeanours, which somehow just adds to the charm.

NEAR NORTH

Bisected by the Magnificent Mile, a stretch of Michigan Avenue packed with upmarket shops and luxury hotels, this is invariably where visitors to the city first land. Some of its most distinctive landmarks are here too. River North is home to an established art community, their galleries and haunts.

WEST LOOP

Chicago's meatpacking district (centred on Fulton Market) and its environs make up the West Loop. The early regenerators included Harpo Studios (Oprah's one-time base). Now the former warehouses are colonised by loft dwellers, galleries, such as Volume (see p035), and fashionable restaurants like Girl & the Goat (see p045).

GOLD COAST

Named after the colour of the money in its residents' coffers, this is where you'll come across some of Chicago's most extravagant mansions, near Astor Street, and lots of high-end shops and restaurants, including Alinea (see p060). Oak Street Beach offers opportunities for some lakeside R&R.

ANDERSONVILLE/LAKE VIEW

North Side neighbourhood Andersonville has emerged as a hotbed for dining and design retail. The primarily residential Lake View absorbs smaller 'hoods like Wrigleyville (see p090) and Boystown, the hub of Chicago's gay scene, at the intersection of Halsted and Clark.

WICKER PARK/LOGAN SQUARE

Favoured by art and music types, Wicker Park is laidback and largely low-rise, full of interesting boutiques and restaurants such as Trenchermen (see p038). Logan Square has been on the up for years, and its great dining rooms and cafés include Gaslight Coffee Roasters (see p048).

LANDMARKS

THE SHAPE OF THE CITY SKYLINE

No other modern city has attempted to create as many landmark structures as Chicago. A collective and corporate will – as well as a certain civic cheerfulness – has seen America's then second, now third, city put up the first skyscrapers and spend the next century sending them ever higher while refining and redefining the form.

It makes for a unique and navigable cityscape, less dense than New York's but unmatched in its historical and stylistic stretch. Two dark giants, the Willis Tower (see po12) and John Hancock Center (see po65), practically bookend downtown. At street level, public art is prevalent; most key buildings have an accompanying sculptural statement, by the likes of Calder, Chagall or Picasso. No surprise, then, that one of the more recent landmarks is a cluster of truly public artwork. In Millennium Park (see po66), Frank Gehry's Jay Pritzker Pavilion, Jaume Plensa's *Crown Fountain* and Anish Kapoor's *Cloud Gate* have become instant icons.

Now further attention is being paid to the waterfront. Studio Gang's boathouses along the river, and the firm's masterplan for the redevelopment of Northerly Island, will transform long-neglected spaces. And, if it ever gets off the ground, Calatrava's lakeside Spire will surely become the totem for a Chicago re-establishing itself as a great American city. Perhaps, as Norman Mailer proclaimed almost 50 years ago, *the* great American city.

For full addresses, see Resources.

Lake Shore Drive apartments

Mies van der Rohe's relocation from Nazi Germany to Chicago was fortuitous in so many ways. One stroke of luck was him meeting developer Herbert Greenwald. Despite Greenwald's youth – he was 31 when they first collaborated in 1946 – he was brave enough to back the architect's vision (although apparently less generous when it came to prompt payments). That vision found almost perfect expression in the four glass towers they put up between 1951 and 1955. The first two, at 860-880 Lake Shore Drive (above), were Mies' first to use glass-and-steel curtain walls with no interior load-bearing walls. The second pair, at No 900-910, are a slightly darker echo of the first two towers. Chicagoans took to the buildings' light and height as if it were their birthright.

860-880 and 900-910 N Lake Shore Drive

Skybridge

In late 2002, this 39-storey building announced, in grand fashion, that there was something happening west of The Loop. The idea was simple: a skyscraper of loft-style apartments with open-plan living areas, lots of natural light and balconies. It works beautifully, because of how the structure has been carefully cut away in order to create 'neighbourhoods' within the building. Skybridge is the creation of Ralph Johnson, Perkins + Will's design principal and one of the most influential architects working in Chicago today; he is also responsible for the hugely successful Boeing HQ (100 N Riverside Plaza). His subsequent, smaller residential tower, The Contemporaine (516 N Wells Street), recalls the big ideas of Skybridge.
1 N Halsted Street,
www.skybridgechicago.com

Willis Tower

Completed in 1973, the 110-storey Willis Tower (formerly the Sears Tower) held the title of the world's tallest building until 1998. The nine bundled towers of different heights, which were conceived by Bruce Graham of Skidmore, Owings & Merrill, and engineer Fazlur Khan, are wonderfully elegant. The cluster design (Graham was allegedly inspired while he was considering the profile of cigarettes popping out of a pack) allows the building to soar. It may have been overtaken by the Petronas Twin Towers in Kuala Lumpur (1998), then Taipei 101 (2004), the Shanghai World Finance Center (2008), Hong Kong's ICC Tower and Dubai's Burj Khalifa (both 2010), but in terms of sheer architectural bravado, the Willis Tower stands alone among the world's super-tall structures.
223 S Wacker Drive, www.willistower.com

Aon Center

Originally known as the Standard Oil Building and nicknamed 'Big Stan', this 346m skyscraper reigned as the city's highest building for just a year after its completion in 1972 (a helicopter had indicated how tall it was going to be at the ground-breaking ceremony). It was overtaken, and then some, by the Willis Tower (see p012). But its position and the gracefulness of Edward Durell Stone's design make it one of Chicago's most emblematic, if not best-loved, towers. The structure was clad in 43,000 marble panels, but when they started to come away in the 1980s, threatening to tumble some 300m, they were replaced with white granite at a cost of more than $60m. The sculptural accompaniment, in the plaza, is a set of metal wind rods by Harry Bertoia.
200 E Randolph Street

Tribune Tower

In 1922, Colonel Robert McCormick, the publisher of the *Chicago Tribune*, launched a contest to design the company's new HQ, and the entries heralded a new age in US architecture. The second-placed entry, by Eliel Saarinen, was a muscular tower with Gothic flourishes that looked eerily like a truncated Empire State Building. (A design by Walter Gropius and Adolf Meyer seems an even more startling premonition of the Chicago to come.) McCormick's winner was less avant-garde – an outsized Gothic fantasy from New York architects Raymond Hood and John Mead Howells. The tower is topped by an almost absurd abstraction of Rouen Cathedral, flying buttresses and all. Now that Chicago boasts more modernism than it knows what to do with, the building is a welcome grand extravagance.

435 N Michigan Avenue

Marina City

An attempt to revitalise Chicago's then struggling city centre, the 1960s 'corn cob' towers are about as charming as 60 storeys of reinforced concrete can be. In a city so rich in superlative buildings, they're up there as totemic mascots (local sons, the band Wilco, put Marina City on the cover of their 2002 album *Yankee Hotel Foxtrot*). The towers were designed by Bertrand Goldberg, who had studied under Mies van der Rohe at the Bauhaus. After returning to Chicago in the 1930s, the young architect developed a very non-Miesian sense of playfulness and distaste for right angles. The arrival of Mies' nearby IBM Building in 1973, now renamed AMA Plaza and home to The Langham hotel (see p027), makes it clear just how much Goldberg had gone his own merry way. *300 N State Street*

HOTELS

WHERE TO STAY AND WHICH ROOMS TO BOOK

Chicago's hotel scene is highly evolved at both the boutique and the luxury ends. There's an embarrassment of choice when it comes to deluxe suites, from The Peninsula (see p024) on the Magnificent Mile, to the Four Seasons (120 E Delaware Place, T 312 280 8800) and The Ritz-Carlton (160 E Pearson Street, T 312 266 1000). Other high-end alternatives are the Sofitel (20 E Chestnut Street, T 312 324 4000) and Park Hyatt (800 N Michigan Avenue, T 312 335 1234). Refurbishments tend to be frequent, so what can be tired one year may have a million-dollar makeover the next.

Despite this being a city at the forefront of modern architecture, local hotel design has been pedestrian in the past. However, things are changing, and there are many accommodations with plenty of added interest. The Langham (see p027) lies within a Mies van der Rohe building (see p015); Hotel Burnham (1 W Washington Street, T 312 782 1111) is a splendid example of 19th-century skyscraping; and the 1929 InterContinental (505 N Michigan Avenue, T 312 944 4100) has a Romanesque pool. Boutique hotels have been growing in number. Where once The James (see p020) was almost alone in this niche, visitors can now choose between Public (opposite), the Waldorf Astoria (see p026), The Wit (see p030) and, more recently, Soho House (see p022). In 2015, Habita makes its Chicago debut in the art deco Northwest Tower (1600-1628 N Milwaukee Avenue). *For full addresses and room rates, see Resources.*

Public

Carved out of Chicago's former, famed Ambassador East Hotel in the Gold Coast district, Public was the first property in a new chain launched by boutique-hotel supremo Ian Schrager. Offering affordable luxury to travellers looking for flawless service, smart design and 21st-century functionality, Schrager fashioned a gem, with Anda Andrei collaborating on the interiors. The lobby has echoes of God's all-white room in *2001: A Space Odyssey*, and the 285 rooms are all unique (Frank Sinatra Suite, above). There's everything you might need: an always-open business centre, a concierge, a gym, in-room spa facilities, a library (overleaf), 24-hour lobby minibar access, gourmet food to go and bike rentals. It's pet-friendly too. *1301 N State Parkway, T 312 787 3700, www.publichotels.com*

The James

Aiming to bridge the gap between the boutique and the luxury hotel categories, Near North's The James has accomplished it with aplomb. The place has a unique, unstuffy air and offers the kind of discreet service that you usually encounter at the old-school end of the market. New York architect Deborah Berke is responsible for the decor – a mix of earth tones, stone and warm timber punctuated with well-placed 20th-century design classics – which helps attract a style-savvy clientele. Each of the 191 rooms and 52 studios (Penthouse Loft, above and opposite) boasts platform beds and spacious marble bathrooms. Chef David Burke hit his stride in the popular steak restaurant Primehouse (T 312 660 6000), while the lavish bar, Jimmy, lures hip cocktail-suppers fresh from a stint of card flexing on the Magnificent Mile.
55 E Ontario Street, T 312 337 1000, www.jameshotels.com

Soho House

The largest of the club's US properties, Chicago's Soho House was wrought out of a historic 1907 warehouse in the West Loop. The building's industrial edge has been enhanced rather than overplayed, and many areas are accessible to the public as well as members, including 40 hotel rooms (Medium Plus, pictured). *113-125 N Green Street, T 312 521 8000, www.sohohousechicago.com*

The Peninsula

Since it opened in 2001, The Peninsula has out-luxed all of its peers. Holding a prime position on the Magnificent Mile, the opulence stretches over 20 floors. The top two are occupied by one of the city's most sophisticated spas and a knockout swimming pool (see p089). The lofty lobby (opposite) exudes grandeur and, between the hours of 8pm and midnight on Fridays and Saturdays, a resolve-melting aroma wafts from a chocolate bar proffering cocoa delicacies. Other treats include Shanghai Terrace, one of the best Asian restaurants in town. Some of the suites, such as The Peninsula (above), have views or studies overlooking Lake Michigan; those on a lower budget may want to choose one of the Junior Suites.
108 E Superior Street, T 312 337 2888, www.peninsula.com/chicago

Waldorf Astoria

Opened as the Elysian, and the recipient of several accolades, including a 2010 Wallpaper* Best Business Hotels award, this Near North property was relaunched as a Waldorf Astoria in 2012. Lisa Simeone and Gina Deary of Simeone Deary Design Group based the hotel's interiors on the decorative styles of the 1920s and 1930s, as is apparent in the glam lobby (above). The 188 rooms are similarly sumptuous,

and done out in a deco-esque style. Retaining its original name, the Elysian Spa & Health Club (T 312 646 1310) offers a host of treatments, as well as fitness facilities. The in-house dining option is an all-day, bistro-like restaurant with a focus on local produce. For a cosy drink, Bernard's Bar is a bijou spot.
11 E Walton Street, T 312 646 1300,
www.waldorfastoriachicagohotel.com

The Langham

Occupying the first 13 floors of Mies van der Rohe's landmark high-rise, completed in 1973 after the architect's death in 1969, the 316-room Langham is a seductive blend of classic modernism and contemporary luxury. Richmond International's interior renovation and decor is pitch-perfect in its chic colour palette and refined materials. The first-floor lobby was entrusted to Mies' grandson, Chicago architect Dirk Lohan, who custom-designed a desk based on a Mies original in Farnsworth House (see p102). The artistic embellishments are a Jaume Plensa sculpture and painting by Enoc Perez. The restaurant, Travelle (T 312 923 7705), is the work of David Rockwell. Opt for a Classic River View Suite (above) and soak up the setting, inside and out.
330 N Wabash Avenue, T 312 923 9988, www.chicago.langhamhotels.com

Reception, The Langham

The Wit
Designed by local architect Jackie Koo,
this upbeat boutique hotel has 298
rooms (Classic King, pictured), whose
interiors are by Cheryl Rowley. The
accommodations are complemented
by an in-house restaurant, bar, 40-seat
cinema and state-of-the-art spa and
gym. The top-floor Roof lounge (T 312
239 9501) affords super city panoramas.
201 N State Street, T 312 467 0200

24 HOURS

SEE THE BEST OF THE CITY IN JUST ONE DAY

Few cities are as defined by their transport systems as Chicago is by the L, or elevated train. The first sections date to 1892, and today the network is slow, crowded and in need of serious investment. But it does allow you to glide two storeys high – a rocking, rickety ride – through the towers of The Loop and out into the various neighbourhoods, some hip and gentrified, others dilapidated and desperate places. A living city, spread out beneath you.

We start in the South Loop, taking in Printers Row (opposite), desolate in the 1970s but now rejuvenated. Next, it's south on the Green Line to 35th-Bronzeville-IIT station, to see the contributions that Rem Koolhaas and Helmut Jahn made to Mies van der Rohe's IIT campus (see p034). Hop back on the Green Line to The Loop, for a shot of caffeine at Intelligentsia (T 312 253 0594) inside the splendid Monadnock Building (53 W Jackson Boulevard), whose interiors deserve a look. Stroll along Jackson, crossing the river into Greektown, then walk up Halsted Street to the meatpacking district. Turn left on to W Washington Boulevard to visit the design gallery Volume (see p035), and two of Chicago's finest contemporary art spaces, Kavi Gupta (see p036) and Andrew Rafacz (No 835, T 312 404 9188). Alternatively, go west to Oak Park, where you can take guided tours of an amazing inventory of houses designed by Frank Lloyd Wright, including his Home and Studio (www.flwright.org). *For full addresses, see Resources.*

10.00 Printers Row

Venture over to South Dearborn to enter a Chicago that feels oddly familiar, especially in the gloom of winter. The streets are so reminiscent of an early gangster movie, it's as if you are trespassing on set. Once the location of nearly 100 printing houses, such as George C Nimmons' 1916 Franklin Building (above; 720 S Dearborn Street), Printers Row degenerated in the late 20th century, but subsequently picked up. Now it's the locale of the city's loft-dwelling literati. Relics endure: of Chicago's six original stations, Dearborn is the solitary survivor, while Kasey's Tavern (T 312 427 7992) has been serving beer since 1889. Call into Sandmeyer's Bookstore (T 312 922 2104), between W Congress Parkway and W Polk Street, and Hackney's (T 312 461 1116), a 1939 mainstay that dishes up an excellent breakfast and brunch.

11.00 Tribune Campus, IIT

Mies van der Rohe put his money where his mouth was during his 20-year tenure as director of architecture at the Illinois Institute of Technology, by designing its campus. However, by the mid-1990s, the IIT began to understand that man cannot live on (or in) Mies alone. Student numbers were down and the college was in need of an architectural shot in the arm. Enter Rem Koolhaas, who won the prize to design the McCormick Tribune Campus Center. He created a long, low building, seemingly squashed by the L train above, wrapped in a 160m corrugated steel-and-concrete tube. IIT asked Helmut Jahn to design the State Street Village student dorms. Strung along the tracks of the L, the stationary sleeper carriages, punctuated with light-filled courtyards, are a triumph.

3300 S Federal Street, www.iit.edu

15.00 Volume Gallery

Founded in 2010, Volume is the brainchild of Sam Vinz and Claire Warner, who met working for Richard Wright (see p084). On a mission to promote contemporary American design, the gallery moved to this permanent West Loop space, amid a clutch of other art spaces, in 2013. Vinz and Warner single out those creatives who, in their view, are forming their own language, and escaping the 'long shadow cast by the great designers of the 20th century'. Past exhibitors have included Jonathan Nesci, Felicia Ferrone, Norman Kelley and Matthias Merkel Hess ('Things', above). The curators promote design collecting, and their gallery is an exemplar of why that should be encouraged. Open Tuesday to Saturday, or by appointment. *Third floor, 845 W Washington Boulevard, T 312 224 8683, www.wvvolumes.com*

16.00 Kavi Gupta Gallery

Former investment banker Kavi Gupta launched his first art gallery in 1997, relocating it to a larger space in 2002. Like next-door gallerist Andrew Rafacz, Gupta champions a high-quality group of artists, such as Chicago-born, Berlin-based painter James Krone ('Waterhome', pictured). Closed Sundays and Mondays.
835 W Washington Boulevard,
T 312 432 0708, www.kavigupta.com

20.00 Trenchermen

Brothers Michael and Patrick Sheerin have been gathering praise as chefs for the past decade, at Blackbird (T 312 715 0708) and The Signature Room (T 312 787 9596) respectively. In 2012, they teamed up with Matt Eisler and Kevin Heisner to launch this bar/restaurant in a 1920 former bathhouse in Wicker Park. Michael has since left to launch Cicchetti (T 312 642 1800) in the Near North, but Trenchermen remains a top-grade dining establishment, with an edge, thanks to Heisner's retro-tinged decor. After schooling from Tona Palomino, Jonah Frank took charge of the bar in 2014. As for the food, we guarantee the unique marriage of flavours, such as Arctic char with sprouted lentils, borscht aioli and horseradish, will impress you. *2039 W North Avenue, T 773 661 1540, www.trenchermen.com*

23.00 Billy Sunday

For the record, before it was the name of one of the city's best craft cocktail bars, Billy Sunday was a baseball player of the late 19th century, who found God at the famous Pacific Garden Mission on Chicago's South Side. The idea for the bar came from Matthias Merges, who also owns the yakitori-led Yusho (T 773 904 8558) and worked with the late chef Charlie Trotter. Together with his wife, Rachel Crowl, who conceived the 1940s-inspired interior, Merges has created an unpretentious outpost in crowded Logan Square. The cocktails are the main event, and they lean towards the sweet, Southern side of the spectrum. The bar comes into its own in winter: cosied up here with a nightcap is an ideal way to see out a bitterly cold day.
3143 W Logan Boulevard, T 773 661 2485, www.billy-sunday.com

URBAN LIFE

CAFÉS, RESTAURANTS, BARS AND NIGHTCLUBS

Foodies won't suffer in Chicago but dieters will struggle. The city is bristling with talented chefs. The most celebrated is molecular gastronomy master Grant Achatz, whose restaurant Alinea (see p060) garnered three Michelin stars in 2010; Achatz also heads up Aviary (see p054). Other cooking heroes include Rick Bayless, Rick Tramonto and pastry chef Gale Gand, who preceded Anthony Martin at Tru (676 N St Clair Street, T 312 202 0001). We're also big fans of Donnie Madia and chef Paul Kahan, who are behind brilliant venues such as Avec (see p044) and The Publican (see p050). Another local restaurant heavyweight, Brendan Sodikoff, is giving them a run for their money (opposite) in the same 'hood.

Chicago does great neighbourhood restaurants. Lula Cafe (2537 N Kedzie Boulevard, T 773 489 9554) is a hip Logan Square hangout known for its seasonal American fare, while Bridgeport's Pleasant House Bakery (964 W 31st Street, T 773 523 7437) is a BYO eaterie focused on pies and desserts. Andersonville, the one-time Swedish district north of Lake View, has recently become something of a dining hotspot. On N Clark Street, check out Marty Fosse's Italian trinity of Anteprima (No 5316, T 773 506 9990), Ombra (No 5310, T 773 506 8600) and Acre (No 5308, T 773 334 7600). Round the corner, try Vincent (1475 W Balmoral Avenue, T 773 334 7168), a charming bistro with a new American menu.

For full addresses, see Resources.

Green Street Smoked Meats

One feather Chicago has in its cap over New York is that it still has a functioning meatpacking district, as opposed to the facade of one. From the 1990s, Oprah Winfrey's Harpo Studios and a string of high-end haunts transformed the near West Loop off Halsted Street into foodie row, but early mornings, it's a bustling, meat-grinding hub. Randolph Street draws Chicagoans for its dining and nightlife, and now food mogul Brendan Sodikoff has joined the fray. Green Street is his Texas-style BBQ joint. The meat comes with a healthy amount of rub and the portions are judicious. On the fence about the ribs or pulled-pork sandwich? Try both and share. If you're suffering meat overload, head to Sodikoff's High Five Ramen in the basement of the same building.
112 N Green Street, T 312 754 0434

Parson's Chicken & Fish

In a city where the weather can be harsh, comfort food goes down well. Parson's Chicken & Fish was launched by the folks behind Longman & Eagle (see p059), and dishes up Southern-inspired fried fare as per the name, along with high-octane cocktails. Despite the hipsters who amass outside at the weekend, the venue is an oasis in Logan Square, with a back porch for summer slumming (you can play ping-pong or shuffleboard out there), and a punchy interior to help lift the winter blues. Order a basket of lightly battered goodness and a cold beer, and settle in to enjoy. There are lighter options on the menu too (small-plate greens, East and West Coast oysters, and a superb chickpea salad with feta cheese and pea shoots).
2952 W Armitage Avenue,
www.parsonschickenandfish.com

Avec

All things considered – the design, the ambience and, of course, the sheer quality of the dishes – Avec is one of our favourite restaurants in the world. An almost severe cedarwood bar with long bench and box seating, it's a no-reservation, squeeze-in-and-tuck-in sort of place, but the top-flight service and food will make you feel right at home. If they're on the menu, try the stuffed medjool dates with smoked bacon and piquillo pepper-tomato sauce, followed by some wood-oven-roasted pork shoulder with pochas beans, cider-braised chorizo and apple. The kitchen stays open until midnight (and until 1am on Fridays and Saturdays); turn up late and you'll find a huddle of the city's best chefs and sommeliers here.
615 W Randolph Street, T 312 377 2002, www.avecrestaurant.com

Girl & the Goat/Little Goat

Stephanie Izard has built a reputation as the creator of some of Chicago's most inventive cuisine. In 2010, she opened her second restaurant, Girl & the Goat, in the meatpacking district. The design, by Karen Herold of 555 International, is a deft reworking of the former industrial space, utilising wooden accents and furnishings, and antique elements. Local produce is key to Izard's cooking, and the menu is split into three sections: fish, meat and vegetables. If you gravitate towards comfort food, head across the street to Little Goat (above), Izard's diner, which is a light, bright antidote to the restaurant. Either is a culinary win-win. *809 W Randolph Street, T 312 492 6262, www.girlandthegoat.com; 820 W Randolph Street, T 312 888 3455, www.littlegoatchicago.com*

Pump Room

Going on eight decades now, the Pump Room has been a gateway for movers and shakers passing through the city. In the golden age of train travel, guests would stay next door, at the Ambassador East Hotel, before making their way to Chicago's version of the Trocadero or Brown Derby in LA. 'Sports jacket required' was the dress code and the venue even made a cameo appearance in Hitchcock's *North by Northwest*. While transforming the Ambassador East into Public (see p017), Ian Schrager replaced Pump Room's faded decor with postmodern interiors by Yabu Pushelberg and lighting by Milan's Dimore Studio. The cooking was entrusted to Jean-Georges Vongerichten, who delivers his unique brand of farm-to-table cuisine. *Public, 1301 N State Parkway, T 312 229 6740, www.pumproom.com*

The Violet Hour

Cocktails and conversation are turned into an art form at this well-concealed lounge in Wicker Park. Since its launch in 2007, the unmarked and windowless exterior has fluctuated between bare wood panels, commissioned graffiti and folk art. Inside, high wingback chairs and curtained partitions create intimate niches, while the sultry decor exudes a speakeasy-meets-Alice in Wonderland aura. Ensconce yourself with a Blushing Lady (Plymouth Gin, lemon, grenadine, egg-white and fig bitters) or a whisky-based Violet Hour Old Fashioned (Elijah Craig 12-year-old, demerara syrup and Angostura bitters). The atmosphere is chic and the house rules commendable: no mobile phone use and no reservations.
1520 N Damen Avenue, T 773 252 1500, www.theviolethour.com

Gaslight Coffee Roasters
Boasting a prime address on a prominent Logan Square corner, Gaslight channels contemporary coffeehouse chic through its semi-industrial interior and quirky collection of taxidermy. Seasonal beans are roasted in-house, and there's a short, European-style food menu (cured meat, cheese, bread) for a quick bite.
2385 N Milwaukee Avenue,
www.gaslightcoffeeroasters.com

The Publican/Publican Quality Meats

Now a cornerstone of Fulton Market's nightlife scene, The Publican is a pork lover's paradise, although there's plenty of seafood too. Communal walnut-wood seating and dozens of lights create a dining experience somewhere between an old banquet hall and a gastropub. Order the charcuterie platter, blood sausage or country ribs, and you'll understand the glowing reviews. If you don't have the time to dig in for a few hours and enjoy a proper tour of the expansive beer and wine lists, pop next door for a snack at sister venue Publican Quality Meats (above), which serves simplified versions of most dishes, to eat in or take away. *837 W Fulton Market, T 312 733 9555, www.thepublicanrestaurant.com; 825 W Fulton Market, T 312 445 8977, www.publicanqualitymeats.com*

Big Star

Modelled on the South-west honky-tonks of the 1930s and 1940s, and housed in a converted garage, Big Star fuses the white- and the blue-collar with its raw yet modish decor of concrete floors and exposed light bulbs. Chicago restaurant luminaries Donnie Madia, Terry Alexander, Peter Garfield and Paul Kahan teamed up to create a taqueria serving Tex Mex: delectable taco de panza (crispy braised pork belly, tomato *guajillo* sauce, *queso fresco*, onion and coriander) and taco de pescado (beer battered tilapia, cabbage, red onion, chipotle mayo, and lime). To accompany the food, there's a range of stellar tequilas, whiskies and beers. When the weather is warm, Big Star's 125-seat patio is an added bonus.
1531 N Damen Avenue, T 773 235 4039, www.bigstarchicago.com

Tanta

River North gets an injection of South American colour at Gastón Acurio's first Midwest venture. An ambassador for Peruvian food, the chef debuted in Lima with wife Astrid, and has since opened restaurants worldwide. His zingy flavours marry nicely with Jeff Zimmerman's pop mural adorning Esyn Design's interior.
118 W Grand Avenue, T 312 222 9700, www.tantachicago.com

Aviary

Grant Achatz's high-concept cocktail den, which operates ticketed drink packages rather than reservations, neighbours his second restaurant, the similarly ticket-based Next (T 312 226 0858). Although Aviary serves small plates, its libations and state-of-the-art cocktail kitchen (which *The Wall Street Journal* described as 'NASA-like' when it launched under Craig Schoettler) are the real attractions.

Charles Joly now mixes the drinks in an open kitchen, which is separated from the lounge by birdcage bars. There are about 30 cocktails, some exquisitely presented in stemware by the Chicago-based artist/designer Martin Kastner, who contributed to the design of Alinea (see p060). If you are lucky, you may get to see The Office, the invitation-only bar in the basement. *955 W Fulton Market, www.theaviary.com*

Cocello

This Italian bar/restaurant in River North is another coup for Brendan Sodikoff, and takes over the space once occupied by another of his eateries, Dillman's. Cocello's menu is built around handmade pasta dishes (*cacio e pepe*, and linguine and clams among them), and small-cut meat and fish dishes, including Tuscan-style beef, stuffed pork belly and grilled fish. The interior design – etched-glass room divider, crystal lights and red-leather banquettes – gives the place a convivial, bistro feel, boosted by the central bar. Imbibe a 'light' or a 'strong' cocktail, some Italian wine, and one of the many amaro-based digestifs. A terrace, as well as early-morning coffee and pastries, and a lunch service, are also planned. *354 W Hubbard Street, T 312 888 9195, www.cocello.com*

The Charleston
This cool neighbourhood tavern was a socialist hangout in the 1930s and barely changed for seven decades. In 2010, Alan Morgensten bought the ageing relic, preserving its homely, storefront feel but adding more of an edge. Weekly live music and a good drinks list make this a splendid place in which to soak up the local vibe.
2076 N Hoyne Avenue, T 773 489 4757

Bavette's Bar & Boeuf

This may be a modern take on the classic Chicago steakhouse, but Bavette's interior is more reminiscent of Musso & Frank, the legendary Hollywood restaurant. It's no wonder. Another triumph for Brendan Sodikoff – alongside the restaurateur's Gilt Bar (T 312 464 9544), Maudes Liquor Bar (T 312 243 9712) and Au Cheval (T 312 929 4580) – its alluring appearance is rooted in the roaring twenties. The hors d'oeuvres menu is packed with seafood and salads, but the main event is the steak. Try the classic Chicago-cut ribeye or filet mignon (petite duchess cut) with roasted tomato, herb butter and cracked pepper. To drink, there's an ample selection of bourbon, whisky, scotch and beer, as well as bubbly and classic cocktails.
218 W Kinzie Street, T 312 624 8154, www.bavetteschicago.com

Longman & Eagle

In the past decade and a half, gastropubs have taken beer-drinking and meat-eating in Chicago to new heights. Logan Square's Longman & Eagle, baby of Peter Toalson, Bruce Finkelstein and the artist/graphic designer Cody Hudson, was one of the trendsetters. Snagging a Michelin star in its first year, 2010, the venue fast became a hipster hangout in a neighbourhood yearning for a new haunt. The cooking is regional American with an emphasis on farm-to-table, and dishes are served as small plates, accompanied by a selection of craft beers and cocktails, and whiskies. There's indoor and outdoor seating in the summer, and if you've had far too much fun, you can always spend the night at the six-room 'inn' upstairs.
2657 N Kedzie Avenue, T 773 276 7110, www.longmanandeagle.com

Alinea

Since Grant Achatz and Nick Kokonas launched Alinea in 2005, it has received so many awards and plaudits that it's hard to believe this establishment lives up to the hype, but it does. There is still no restaurant in the country quite like it, and presentation is paramount. From the elaborate multi-course (up to 20) meals, with optional wine pairings, to the sculptures and the extravagant serviceware by Martin Kastner, this is contemporary haute cuisine at its finest. For the best summary of what Alinea has to offer, we recommend the prix-fixe menu. You have to plan ahead if you want to dine here – instead of taking reservations, Alinea operates a pre-paid ticketing system on its website.
1723 N Halsted Street, T 312 867 0110, www.alinea-restaurant.com

Acadia

A 2012 addition to the thriving South Loop corridor, and only a few blocks from Lake Michigan, Acadia is divided into a lounge, a dining room and a private salon. The restaurant's elegant furnishings and soft neutral hues make for a sophisticated setting. Chef/proprietor Ryan McCaskey's revolving menu is sparse, but underscores his contemporary take on classic American cuisine. One of the most talked-about items on his menu has been the lobster pot pie: butter-poached lobster pieces, Tokyo turnips and potato-dauphinoise balls flavoured with tarragon, with a sour-cream pastry top and side serving of lobster bisque. Leading the haute-cuisine charge in the South Loop, Acadia has already earned one Michelin star.
1639 S Wabash Avenue, T 312 360 9500, www.acadiachicago.com

INSIDER'S GUIDE

MICHAEL RENAUD, CREATIVE DIRECTOR

Head creative for music website Pitchfork (www.pitchfork.com), its festivals and quarterly print publication, *The Pitchfork Review*, Michael Renaud is a deep fan of his hometown: 'Chicago is modest about its achievements, which many would fault as a Midwest mentality, but I think it's more about getting satisfaction from doing good work than taking the credit for it. Chicago has class.'

Logan Square, the neighbourhood where Renaud resides and works, is, in his view, one of the foremost dining destinations in town, but he suggests exploring other districts too, like Pilsen and Bridgeport. In Pilsen's landmark 1890 Thalia Hall (1227 W 18th Street, T 312 526 3851), there's a music venue, standout gastropub, Dusek's, and cool bar, Punch House. In the same area, Nightwood (2119 S Halsted Street, T 312 526 3385) and Nana (3267 S Halsted Street, T 312 929 2486) are 'incredible food options'. Gaslight (see p048), Ipsento (2035 N Western Avenue, T 773 904 8177) and Bow Truss (406 N Wells Street) are Renaud's tips for a top cup of joe.

'Sundown's a great time to tour downtown,' he says, 'on a bike hired from one of the city's Divvy stations (www.divvybikes.com). There's little traffic, and coasting amid world-class architecture as if you have it all to yourself is a great feeling. Reserve a spot at Three Dots and a Dash (435 N Clark Street, T 312 610 4220), Paul McGee's tiki bar, an oasis in the somewhat touristy River North.' *For full addresses, see Resources.*

ARCHITOUR

A GUIDE TO CHICAGO'S ICONIC BUILDINGS

In 1871, much of Chicago was destroyed by fire. For a city already committed to challenging New York as the commercial (if not the cultural) epicentre of the nation, this provided Chicago with the chance to rebuild itself as a dynamic metropolis, and architects poured in from all over the country to be part of the grand project. Among them were Louis Henry Sullivan – who devised the maxim 'form follows function' – William Le Baron Jenney, Daniel Burnham and his partner John Root. They developed what became known as the Chicago School and built the first skyscrapers here. Although they barely made it into double digits, storey-wise, these buildings were, in their steel-frame construction and emphasis on functional styling, the technical parents of the giants to come.

Chicago seems to provide textbook illustrations of successive architectural styles. The city gave the world the vertical thrust of the skyscraper and the horizontal planes of the Prairie School; it was the mother lode of modernism and then a PoMo playground. And these shifts from one style to another can appear seamless. Of course, the development of its architecture has always been the result of a fierce and chaotic contest of different approaches and interests – sometimes in the same building. It is the quality of the competition that makes Chicago the city where 20th-century architecture was defined and where it found its most perfect form. *For full addresses, see Resources.*

John Hancock Center

One firm, Skidmore, Owings & Merrill, has dominated corporate architecture in postwar America. Nowhere is that more evident than in Chicago. And no building better exemplifies SOM's power slabs than the John Hancock Center, completed in 1970. Largely the work of architect Bruce Graham, and engineers Fazlur Khan and Myron Goldsmith, the uncompromising crisscross trusses and black aluminium skin of the tapered 344m-high, 100-storey tower give it a brooding, iconic force, and make it the definitive Chicago building. The John Hancock Center marks one end of the Magnificent Mile and the open-air viewing deck on the 94th floor is one of the finest places to take in the vistas of Chicago and an impressive portion of the Midwest.
*875 N Michigan Avenue, T 312 751 3681,
www.johnhancockcenterchicago.com*

Millennium Park

The most controversial of former mayor Richard M Daley's civic improvements, the 2004 Millennium Park takes up 10 hectares and is dominated by massive sculptural statements, one of which is Frank Gehry's Jay Pritzker Pavilion (pictured). The giant steel petals and intricate piping canopy of this open-air auditorium play perfectly to the architect's strengths.

201 E Randolph Street, T 312 742 1168

Trump Tower

When tycoon Donald Trump announced that he was going to build in the middle of downtown, along the river, many scoffed at the New Yorker's gaudiness when it came to funding cheaply produced, forgettable high-rises. But as the SOM/Adrian Smith-designed tower rose, so did expectations. When it was finished in 2009, a decent number of architecture buffs warmed to the 423m structure, which echoes Smith's Burj Khalifa in Dubai. This 92-storey glass-and-steel behemoth replaced the drab Chicago Sun-Times building, one of the biggest architectural eyesores in the city. However, the 6m-high 'Trump' sign the magnate emblazoned on the riverside facade in 2014 has been less well received, and has caused a public kerfuffle.
401 N Wabash Avenue, T 312 588 8000, www.trumpchicagohotel.com

Lake Point Tower

George Schipporeit and John Heinrich's 1968 high-rise is still one of the chicest addresses in town, and its design is as compelling now as then. Essentially, the 70-storey tower has a triangular plan with bowed sides. All the supports and services are at the core, meaning that none of the promontories requires any interior load-bearing walls, which allows for complete freedom of design. Each apartment has a view of Lake Michigan but, thanks to the curvature of the windows, not of other residents' homes. The building also has a 10,000 sq m private park on the third floor. Designed by the landscape architect Alfred Caldwell, it includes an outdoor swimming pool, a waterfall and lagoon, manicured gardens and some 80 trees. *505 N Lake Shore Drive, www.lakepointtower.org*

The Rookery

At the end of the 1800s, Chicago was a Beijing or a Shanghai: architects moved there to erect a new metropolis. Among them were Daniel Burnham and John Root. The 1888 Rookery is their finest and most influential work. The tallest building in the world when it was finished, it has an extraordinary exterior representing a mix of Venetian, Moorish and Byzantine styles. But it's the interior that was truly radical. An atrium and a large light well allowed for an indoor shopping arcade (the first of its kind), and the lobby has elaborate staircases, ornamental rails and carved marble panels. Frank Lloyd Wright renovated the central courtyard in 1905, and after falling into disrepair, the building has now been beautifully restored.
209 S LaSalle Street,
therookerybuilding.com

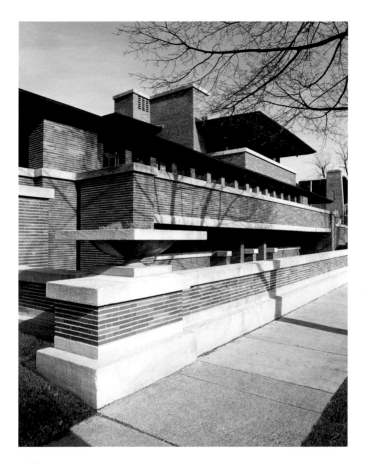

Robie House

Finished in 1910, Robie House is the most famous and fully realised of Frank Lloyd Wright's Prairie houses. Frederick Robie was a bicycle-factory owner – a forward-thinking entrepreneur who wanted the most modern home possible. And the one that Wright designed and built for him was revolutionary, not least in having burglar alarms, a built-in vacuum cleaner and a connected garage. The house resembles an angular, futuristic ship, dry-docked in one of South Chicago's most upmarket neighbourhoods. Everything, down to the choice of brick, is designed to emphasise the horizontal planes. The building, which is open to the public, has been undergoing a multimillion-dollar renovation, and the major structural work is now complete.
5757 S Woodlawn Avenue,
T 312 994 4000, www.flwright.org

Joe and Rika Mansueto Library

Blair Kamin, the *Chicago Tribune*'s
architecture critic, likened Helmut
Jahn's 2011 library at the University of
Chicago to a sci-fi film set. Jahn's orb-
like dome juts out of the ground near
the Midway quad, flooding the Grand
Reading Room (pictured) with natural
light. The furniture was designed by
London-based architect Yorgo Lykouria.
1100 E 57th Street

Metropolitan Correctional Center

Possibly the most startling structure in all of Chicago, which is saying something, the Metropolitan Correctional Center is a slit-windowed fortress of the future, the prison from a grim science-fiction movie landed at the southern edge of The Loop. Designed by Harry Weese, who was also responsible for the metro system in Washington DC, and completed in 1975, it's an innovative 27-storey triangular concrete wedge (the prison occupies 16 floors and the rest of the building is office space). At the time, it represented the latest in correctional best practice and compassionate incarceration; the design meant that all cells had windows but could also be near the facility's well-appointed communal areas. Yet it still appears thoroughly dystopian – in a cool way.
71 W Van Buren Street

Aqua Tower

Completed in 2010, the Aqua is the most distinctive structure erected in the city since the first edition of this book was published in 2007, and has won several architectural awards. Designed by Studio Gang, led by Illinois native Jeanne Gang, the 82-storey mixed-use skyscraper has a wave-like facade, which cascades from top to bottom, producing awe-inspiring views of the building from street level.

Sustainability was a crucial factor in the design and choice of materials; Gang and her team conceived terrace extensions to maximise solar shading, built rainwater collection systems to tackle spillage, and used energy-efficient lighting throughout. Moreover, Aqua's green roof is the largest in Chicago. Gang also came in bang on budget, despite all the eco features.
225 N Columbus Drive

Fisher Studio Houses

Still an incredibly successful splice of art deco design and modernist mechanics, the 1936 Fisher Studio Houses were conceived by Andrew Rebori, a noted bon vivant who had useful relations with Chicago's social elite. The project was commissioned by Frank Fisher Jr, an executive at Marshall Field & Co. Fisher showed Rebori a very narrow plot and told him to get the most (upscale) apartments he could out of it.

Rebori devised a plan for 12 four-storey duplexes built around a courtyard. They were fronted by an elegant painted-brick and rounded glass-brick facade – typical of the 'Depression modern' school – with sculptural flourishes by artist Edgar Miller. Indeed, there is a suspicion that Miller had a larger hand in the building's design and it remains a thrilling composition face on.
1209 N State Parkway

Chase Tower

As many splendid buildings as there are in Chicago, there are also a good many clunkers. Luckily, the central block of The Loop, a symbolic focal point, is occupied by one of the city's most dramatic and graceful constructions. Originally called First National Bank Building and, pretty soon after, Bank One Plaza, Chase Tower was designed by CF Murphy Associates and Perkins + Will, and was completed in 1969. A 60-storey modernist slab, its intense visual drama is the result of an elegant sweep from the base, which starts at 61m wide, to the top, where the structure ends up only half that. The tower is also known for the two-storey sunken plaza to its south, which includes Marc Chagall's *Four Seasons*, a mosaic rendered in 370 sq m of ceramic tiles.
10 S Dearborn Street

Gary Comer Youth Center
Situated in the tough Grand Crossing
neighbourhood, this youth centre was
designed as an inspirational symbol and
resource for a community struggling
with big problems. Most of the building
is made up of long blue or red panelled
bricks — architect John Ronan was
instructed not to use too much glass.
7200 S Ingleside Avenue,
www.gcychome.org

SHOPPING

THE BEST RETAIL THERAPY AND WHAT TO BUY

Newcomers to Chicago may anticipate a paucity of unique retail opportunities, but the city is a robust shopping destination. It has become a mecca for enthusiasts of midcentury design (see p084 and p087), and its booming food culture has put gastro-gadgetry on the agenda; we recommend Medinah Home (600 N Wabash Avenue, T 312 324 7500) and Olivia's Market (2014 W Wabansia Avenue, T 773 227 4220). There's a vibrant coffee scene, and while local brand Intelligentsia (see p032) rules the roast, we also like the pleasingly packaged Metropolis line, which can be sampled in the brand's Edgewater outlet (1039 W Granville Avenue, T 773 764 0400) and bought online (www.metropoliscoffee.com).

Shopping can be split into areas. On the north side of W Fulton Street in the West Loop is a strip of design stores, including Morlen Sinoway Atelier (1052 W Fulton Market, T 312 432 0100). A little to the north is vintage emporium Modern Times (see p087) and, in the Ukrainian Village, Circa Modern (1114 N Ashland Avenue, T 773 697 9239). Wicker Park, Bucktown and Lake View are best for independent fashion stores, while the upscale brands can be found along the Magnificent Mile and the wallet-weakening area around Oak Street. For art of the established variety, River North is the place, whereas Peoria Street has a more contemporary edge. The south end of The Loop has good one-off bookstores.
For full addresses, see Resources.

Sung Jang

A graduate of Milan's Domus Academy and the School of the Art Institute of Chicago, designer Sung Jang says his creativity is rooted in this city. His studies in fine arts and sculpture inform his work, which is as much about process and the perceived quality of a design as the finished object. The '03' stool (above), from $800, is part of his 'Comb Pattern' collection. A firm supporter of Chicago's manufacturing heritage, the designer chose a milling technique that creates unique patterns on the seat, produced in a variety of hardwoods; the legs are made of maple. Jang describes the local design scene as going from strength to strength, due to galleries like Volume (see p035), which he works with, and initiatives such as the Chicagoland collective.
www.sungjanglaboratory.com

Gallery Aesthete
This sleek showroom, opened in 2012
by Stephen Naparstek and designed
by Lukas Machnik, sells accessories,
objets d'art and menswear. Alongside
cult labels like Boris Bidjan Saberi and
Julius, the shop features artists' work
on a rotating basis. Attendant opening
and closing events are held in store.
*Fourth floor, 46 E Oak Street, T 312 265
1883, www.galleryaesthete.com*

Wright Gallery

Some of the rarest pieces of modernist
design find their way to this West Loop
warehouse, before being redistributed
under the hammer to a widely flung
community of collectors. Here you can
bid for a Robert Mallet-Stevens armchair,
a Poul Kjærholm coffee table, or even a
Pierre Koenig Case Study House – items
that fetch huge sums and are right at the
heart of the 'Is it art/Is it design?' debate.
Created by Richard Wright in a one-time
printers, the space has been adapted
to the business. Pieces arrive through a
shuttered door, are transferred to a photo
studio to be documented, then moved to
the display area (right). On auction days,
a café is set up in the mezzanine viewing
gallery – peer over the side and you'll
spy spectacular midcentury furnishings
stacked in the storage room.
1440 W Hubbard Street, T 312 563 0020,
www.wright20.com

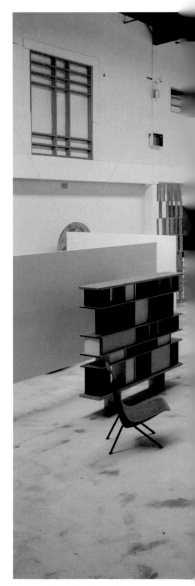

Tusk

Mary Eleanor Wallace is a nurse who hails from the South. After finding her way to Chicago, she launched a boutique in her spare time, themed around her interests: art, objets, fashion and design (her mother and grandmother were antiques dealers). Wallace named her shop Tusk, she told us, simply because she liked the word: 'short, harsh and elegant at the same time'. Her well-edited stock has more than a hint of the West Coast about it, but also feels spot on in contemporary Chicago, displayed in a beautifully restored, early 20th century storefront in Logan Square. Every item has a backstory, and Wallace is on hand, from Thursday to Sunday, to tell you about it. She's currently working on developing new collaborations and one-off pieces.
3205 W Armitage Road, T 423 903 7093, www.tuskchicago.com

Modern Times

Occupying a vast brick-walled warehouse space, Modern Times is at the western frontier of the design district. Tom Clark and Martha Torno opened their gallery of 20th-century pieces back in 1991, and their hoard remains as strong as ever. Rich in American midcentury modern lighting, ceramics and furnishings, this impressive collection is low on design clichés and high on more unusual finds, including items by under-the-radar designers and artisanal work produced in the Chicago area. Everything on sale is in tip-top condition, so it's well worth trekking out here. A personal passion for vintage accessories is reflected in the couple's sideline (www.modbag.com), bags and jewels sourced on their travels. *2100 W Grand Avenue, T 312 243 5706, www.moderntimeschicago.com*

SPORTS AND SPAS
WORK OUT, CHILL OUT OR JUST WATCH

To the uninitiated, the sporting landscape of Chicago may appear to be populated by animals you wouldn't want to encounter on a dark night: bears and bulls among them. But these are the stars of the city's stadia. The Cubs (Wrigley Field, see p090) and White Sox (Cellular Field) are the leading baseball teams; the Bears are Chicago's representatives on the gridiron; the Blackhawks play ice hockey; and the Bulls are the basketball team that won six NBA titles in the 1990s under the leadership of Michael Jordan. The arenas hold their own as well. For the best of the old visit Wrigley Field, and for the best of the new check out the Bears' renovated Soldier Field (1410 S Museum Campus Drive, T 312 235 7152).

When it comes to everyday corporeal honing, the city has parks and lakeshore trails for runners and cyclists. Gyms and spas are plentiful, if mostly undistinguished in design. The pool at the Four Seasons (see p016) has throwaway swimming costumes and an enviable ceiling view, but The Peninsula Spa pool (opposite) is preferable for lengths. The city's most enticing pampering retreat is the Cowshed Spa at Soho House (see p022), which is open to the public and offers quick-service facilities for men and women, in addition to its signature organic treatments. Meanwhile, David Barton Gym (see p092) and Sparrow salon (see p094) satisfy our desire to feel a sense of place when working out or being coiffed. *For full addresses, see Resources.*

The Peninsula Spa

The esteemed Peninsula hotel (see p024) can't rest on its laurels without risking a fall. Which explains why, within five years of the launch in the early noughties, the in-house spa underwent a rejig to turn it into one of the city's most attractive urban retreats. The serene space takes up the top two floors of the building. The reception and treatment areas are both wrapped in wood, a high-tech gym surveys Lake Michigan from a distance of 20 floors up, and the 25m pool (above), which has floor-to-ceiling glass windows on the 19th storey, is the longest in any downtown hotel. There's also a terrace for summer idling, a yoga studio and a wide-ranging therapy list using Espa products. The spa is open to non-guests seven days a week.
108 E Superior Street, T 312 573 6860, www.peninsula.com/chicago

Wrigley Field

One of the country's oldest and best-loved ballparks, Wrigley Field was built in 1914 for a now defunct Federal League team, the Whales. Situated at the intersection of Clark and Addison, the park dominates the northern side of the Wrigleyville neighbourhood, not least when there's a game on and the surrounding streets and rooftops are filled with fans. The architect, Zachary Taylor Davis, was a contemporary of Frank Lloyd Wright, and both worked as draughtsmen for Louis Henry Sullivan. Whereas previous ballparks had tended to be temporary wooden structures, Davis introduced steel beams and concrete. Renovated by chewing-gum magnate William Wrigley Jr in the 1920s, the advertisement-free, ivy-covered, asymmetric stadium has changed little since the 1940s.

1060 W Addison Street, T 773 404 2827, chicago.cubs.mlb.com

David Barton Gym

Spread over more than 3,000 sq m, the Chicago outpost of fitness entrepreneur David Barton is located inside the 1908 Montgomery Ward Building, which was once the headquarters of the world's largest mail-order company. The interior comes courtesy of William Sofield, who retained the warehouse feel by utilising 1940s street lamps and exposed concrete pillars, softened by whimsical touches such as bright orange flokati on the walls, cushion-strewn banquettes and televisions screening images of log fires. Johnson Schwinghammer's lighting is designed to flatter gym bunnies working up a sweat. The facilities include a spin studio and two steam rooms, and personal trainers and masseurs are on hand.
600 W Chicago Avenue, T 312 836 9127, www.davidbartongym.com

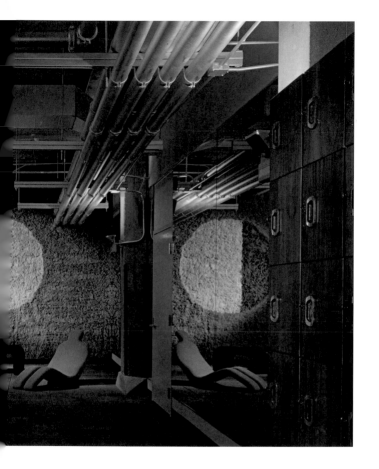

Sparrow
A good reason to have your hair cut in Logan Square, Bathsheba Nemerovski and Susan Flaga's Sparrow is housed in an 1882 building that once functioned as an old-school barbershop. The super-trendy salon has preserved some of the original wallpaper, sinks and tin-roof ceilings. An appointment is a must.
2545 N Milwaukee Avenue,
T 773 486 9300, www.sparrowhair.com

ESCAPES

WHERE TO GO IF YOU WANT TO LEAVE TOWN

Despite Chicago's status as one of the world's busiest aviation hubs, few think of it as a base for shorter jaunts. This is despite the fact that much of the surrounding country is not the flat, grassy prairie of legend, but rather hills and beaches, sand dunes and great pine forests. It is no accident that immigrant Scandinavians have found such comfort in the local landscape. Visitors have four states to explore: Illinois, Michigan, Wisconsin and Indiana, each with its own particular and peculiar history. Berrien County, 150km to the north-east, has become a focal point for Michigan's surprisingly vibrant viticulture. Nearby Harbor County boasts the upscale New Buffalo lakeside resort. Madison, Wisconsin's capital, is known for its 260 parks, five lakes, 10 beaches, fine food, vigorous cultural life and all-round liveability. And it's just 240km away.

The Midwest also does a nice line in built environment. It is as if the architectural energy expended on Chicago spread, from Mies van der Rohe's impeccable Farnsworth House (see p102) in Plano, Illinois, and Frank Lloyd Wright's monumental efforts in Racine, Wisconsin (see p100), to the unique result of corporate benevolence in Columbus, Indiana (opposite and p098). If that isn't enough, there's Santiago Calatrava's Milwaukee Art Museum (700 N Art Museum Drive, Milwaukee, T 414 224 3200). And you thought all the city had to offer was beer and *Laverne & Shirley*. *For full addresses, see Resources.*

Columbus, Indiana

Despite having a population of just 44,000, Columbus has been anointed as the sixth-most architecturally significant city in the US. In 1957, the town's major employer, the Cummins Engine Company (run by J Irwin Miller, the 'Medici of the West'), decided it would cover the design fees for a series of public buildings, as long as the architects were of international standing and modernist intent. There had been a precursor: Eero Saarinen's 1954 Irwin Union Bank, which broke the mould for finance buildings in America. To date, Columbus has more than 60 edifices of interest, including Saarinen's 1957 Miller House (overleaf) and 1964 North Christian Church (above), as well as works by IM Pei, Robert Venturi and Deborah Berke. The Columbus Area Visitors Center (T 812 378 2622) runs various architectural tours.

Miller House, Columbus, Indiana
This family home, commissioned by
J Irwin and his wife, Xenia Simons Miller,
is one of America's finest modernist
residences. Eero Saarinen's flowing,
grid-plan design, lit by a series of
skylights, was enhanced by Alexander
Girard's furnishings, including an
innovative 'storage wall' (pictured).
Landscape architect Dan Kiley created
the exquisitely formed gardens.

Johnson Wax Building, Racine

Despite a reputation as a huge, if irascible, architectural talent, Frank Lloyd Wright was struggling with a lack of work in the mid-1930s. He was rescued by HF Johnson Jr of SC Johnson, the wax people, who commissioned him to build new offices, and a mansion, in the lakeside town of Racine, Wisconsin. Completed in 1939, the office building is a squat, corporate-sized take on the Prairie Style, and it became known for its mushroom-like 9.5m internal columns (opposite). Despite the infamous Wright temper, Johnson approached him again, to design a research facility. The architect came up with a 15-storey tower (above), opened in 1950, which is still a wonder to behold. Sadly, it closed after three decades, but it is now open for free public tours. *1525 Howe Street, T 262 260 2154*

Farnsworth House, Plano

Mies van der Rohe never got more Miesian (or more grief) than he did for Farnsworth House, completed in 1951. The client was Dr Edith Farnsworth, a kidney specialist from Chicago who asked the architect to design and build her a country house on a 25-hectare plot on the Fox River in Plano, Illinois. He came up with a sublime floating glazed box, measuring just 23.5m by 8.8m, held aloft by white steel I-beams. Not that Dr Farnsworth was content. She kicked Mies off the job before he had completed the interiors and sued for incompetence. There is, however, some suspicion that the relationship between Mies and the good doctor went beyond the professional, and that she was far from pleased when the master architect's ardour cooled.
14520 River Road, T 630 552 0052,
www.farnsworthhouse.org

NOTES
SKETCHES AND MEMOS

RESOURCES
CITY GUIDE DIRECTORY

The Publican 050
837 W Fulton Market
T 312 733 9555
www.thepublicanrestaurant.com

Publican Quality Meats 050
825 W Fulton Market
T 312 445 8977
www.publicanqualitymeats.com

Pump Room 046
Public
1301 N State Parkway
T 312 229 6740
www.pumproom.com

R

Robie House 071
5757 S Woodlawn Avenue
T 312 994 4000
www.flwright.org

Roof 030
The Wit
201 N State Street
T 312 239 9501
www.thewithotel.com

The Rookery 070
209 S LaSalle Street
therookerybuilding.com

S

Sandmeyer's Bookstore 033
714 S Dearborn Street
T 312 922 2104
www.sandmeyersbookstore.com

The Signature Room 038
John Hancock Center
875 N Michigan Avenue
T 312 787 9596
www.signatureroom.com

Skybridge 011
1 N Halsted Street
www.skybridgechicago.com

Soldier Field 088
1410 S Museum Campus Drive
T 312 235 7152
www.soldierfield.net

Sparrow 094
2545 N Milwaukee Avenue
T 773 486 9300
www.sparrowhair.com

T

Tanta 052
118 W Grand Avenue
T 312 222 9700
www.tantachicago.com

Thalia Hall 062
1227 W 18th Street
T 312 526 3851
www.thaliahallchicago.com

Three Dots and a Dash 062
435 N Clark Street
T 312 610 4220
www.threedotschicago.com

Travelle 027
The Langham
330 N Wabash Avenue
T 312 923 7705
www.chicago.langhamhotels.com

Trenchermen 038
2039 W North Avenue
T 773 661 1540
www.trenchermen.com

HOTELS
ADDRESSES AND ROOM RATES

Hotel Burnham 016
Room rates:
double, from $510
1 W Washington Street
T 312 782 1111
www.burnhamhotel.com

Four Seasons 016
Room rates:
double, from $270
120 E Delaware Place
T 312 280 8800
www.fourseasons.com/chicagofs

InterContinental 016
Room rates:
double, from $300
505 N Michigan Avenue
T 312 944 4100
www.icchicagohotel.com

The James 020
Room rates:
double, from $260;
Penthouse Loft, from $1,200
55 E Ontario Street
T 312 337 1000
www.jameshotels.com

The Langham 027
Room rates:
double, from $395;
Classic River View Suite, from $1,000
330 N Wabash Avenue
T 312 923 9988
www.chicago.langhamhotels.com

Longman & Eagle 059
Room rates:
double, from $85
2657 N Kedzie Avenue
T 773 276 7110
www.longmanandeagle.com

Park Hyatt 016
Room rates:
double, from $315
800 N Michigan Avenue
T 312 335 1234
www.parkchicago.hyatt.com

The Peninsula 024
Room rates:
double, from $625;
Junior Suite, from $1,150;
Peninsula Suite, $9,000
108 E Superior Street
T 312 337 2888
www.peninsula.com/chicago

Public 017
Room rates:
double, from $275;
Frank Sinatra Suite, $675
1301 N State Parkway
T 312 787 3700
www.publichotels.com

The Ritz-Carlton 016
Room rates:
double, from $295
160 E Pearson Street
T 312 266 1000
www.fourseasons.com/chicagorc

Sofitel 016
Room rates:
double, from $395
20 E Chestnut Street
T 312 324 4000
www.sofitel.com

Soho House 022
Room rates:
double, from $160;
Medium Plus, from $320
113-125 N Green Street
T 312 521 8000
www.sohohousechicago.com

Waldorf Astoria 026
Room rates:
double, from $350
11 E Walton Street
T 312 646 1300
www.waldorfastoriachicagohotel.com
The Wit 030
Room rates:
double, from $120;
Classic King Room, from $120
201 N State Street
T 312 467 0200
www.thewithotel.com

WALLPAPER* CITY GUIDES

Executive Editor
Rachael Moloney

Authors
Nick Compton
JC Gabel

Art Editor
Eriko Shimazaki
Original Design
Loran Stosskopf
Map Illustrator
Russell Bell

Photography Editor
Elisa Merlo
Assistant Photography Editor
Nabil Butt

Production Manager
Vanessa Todd-Holmes

Chief Sub-Editor
Nick Mee

Editorial Assistant
Emilee Jane Tombs

Contributor
Emma Moore

Intern
Marina Hartung

Wallpaper* ® is a
registered trademark
of IPC Media Limited

First published 2007
Revised and updated
2012, 2013 and 2014

© Phaidon Press Limited

All prices are correct at
the time of going to press,
but are subject to change.

Printed in China

Phaidon Press Limited
Regent's Wharf
All Saints Street
London N1 9PA

Phaidon Press Inc
65 Bleecker Street
New York, NY 10012

Phaidon® is a registered
trademark of Phaidon
Press Limited

www.phaidon.com

A CIP Catalogue record for
this book is available from
the British Library.

ISBN 978 0 7148 6824 0

PHOTOGRAPHERS

CHICAGO
A COLOUR-CODED GUIDE TO THE HOT 'HOODS

THE LOOP
Innovative builds at every turn include the world's first, and some of its finest, skyscrapers

LINCOLN PARK
Chicago's gilded youth have made this area their own, although its light is fading now

SOUTH LOOP
Capone-era warehouses loom over a renascent district of bars, bookshops and eateries

NEAR NORTH
The Magnificent Mile has to be the first port of call for any self-respecting retail junkie

WEST LOOP
From meatpackers to media types, the former industrial zone is now a hip hangout

GOLD COAST
Spectacular residential architecture marks the addresses of the Windy City's wealthy

ANDERSONVILLE/LAKE VIEW
This amalgamation of districts includes sporty Wrigleyville and gay village Boystown

WICKER PARK/LOGAN SQUARE
Pretty townhouses and relaxed caffeine pitstops attract a cool and creative crowd

For a full description of each neighbourhood, see the Introduction.
Featured venues are colour-coded, according to the district in which they are located.